The Greenleaf Guide to
Famous Men of
Rome

by Cyndy A. Shearer

Greenleaf Press
Lebanon, Tennessee

3761 Highway 109 N., Unit D,
Lebanon, TN 37087
Phone: 615-449-1617

History for the thoughtful child

HOW TO USE THIS GUIDE

Introduction:

When you want to build something, a hammer is a very useful thing to have. But if someone picks up your hammer and starts beating you over the head with it, the hammer is no longer a tool — it's a murder weapon. So it is with text books and study guides. This book is intended to be a tool, a possible model for you to use and adapt as you see fit. You will know what suggestions will work best for the students you teach. I hope you will find it useful.

Putting your study in context:

Before you begin your study of this book, let me suggest that you put it in context — not so much chronological context as biblical. Before our family began to study <u>Famous Men of Rome</u> we went back to the Old Testament and reviewed the first few chapters of Genesis and reread the descriptions of those who followed Adam and sons. We made note of who were the farmers, who were herdsmen, who were workers in what craft. The picture that we saw there was very different from the typical evolutionary picture of homosapiens gradually leaving his primitive life as "hunter-gatherer" to settle down into more advanced stationary lifestyle. Read through the story of the Tower of Babel. Discuss what you read together with the children you teach.

Once we had covered this material, we turned to the first chapter of Romans and read about what happens when man turns away from the truth and exchanges it for a lie. Again, we saw that the Bible paints a very different picture of the "evolution of religion" than that which is presented by evolutionary doctrines. Evolution teaches that man crawled out of the primordial mush a primitive animist. Our ancestors then gradually evolved to higher, more sophisticated forms of religion — becoming, first, polytheists and then monotheists (next step atheists?). The Bible, however teaches just the opposite — that created man understood that there was one God, but as men turned away, rejecting truth, God turned them over to lies. Man exchanged the truth of monotheism for the lies of polytheism and animism.

So when you look at the early history of nations, you often find an initial mix of myth, legends, and history. (The weapon used so often against college Christians... "Ah," they often say, "You see, all the cultures of the world have the same myths that the primitive Hebrews had....) So it is important to talk about what the differences and similarities are between myth, legend, and history. When you read the creation stories of other nations the differences between them and the Biblical record of creation are glaring.

We read the myths and legends of Rome and talked about the characteristics of the gods and goddesses. What should we expect the Roman culture/people to be like, based on what we observed about their religion? Who were their heroes? What were they like? We could do this because we had started with Genesis (knew how people developed different skills...different nations), and because we had started with Paul's Letter to the Romans and talked about the devolution of religion. And I don't recommend teaching mythology outside of this context.

Suggestions for Teacher Preparation:

1. Familiarize yourself with the chronology at the back of this study guide, so that you have a sense of where you are going to begin and end. This will also briefly introduce you to the names of some of the people you will be reading about.

2. Read through the **Famous Men** text for yourself and the study guide's lessons and assignments before you begin teaching them.

Methods of Evaluation:

When we think of testing, we usually think of exams — essay questions, true/false, multiple choice. There is a place for traditional testing both in and out of conventional classroom settings, but don't overlook the other options. If after reading a story, or listening to you read it aloud, the child is able to tell you the story in his own words — you can know that he understands it. That's really the reason for testing... to make sure your student understands the material.

Another means by which you can evaluate a student's understanding of a selection is through oral discussion. The "For Discussion" questions provided for each chapter are intended to be suggestions — questions you might ask. Often, as you discuss the reading, you will naturally cover the material without sticking to a rigid "question/answer" format. Treasure those times! Sometimes you will need to draw your students along point by point. Sometimes you will need to ask questions different from those suggested. By all means, do.

Written assignments also help evaluate understanding. Some "For Discussion" questions will work particularly well as essay topics. Occasionally have your students retell the story by presenting it as a news story, short story, play, etc.

Many chapters in the book contain legends or stories told about famous figures and are included because they demonstrate some character trait or attitude valued by or typical of the people of the nation. It is not necessary to approach these chapters in the same way you might approach a chapter about someone like Julius Caesar. There are certain battles, facts, dates and people that make good historical memory work. All chapters are not created equal in this regard.

Summary:

Our goals for the study of history are these:

1. That our students will see that God is involved in all history.
    Because God is involved in all of life, Scripture is relevant to all of life. Therefore, all things can and should be evaluated in light of Scripture. As we look at how men and women in our history have made choices, we have a unique opportunity to evaluate those choices as we see what kinds of endings they made for themselves. We can then consider what kind of lives we are building for ourselves and modeling for our children. In this way we can use history as a means by which God can teach us to number <u>our</u> days and apply <u>our</u> hearts to wisdom.

2. That when our students begin to study history in advanced courses they will not be starting from scratch, but will be building on a well-laid foundation.
    They will have a general knowledge of important people and events and have a good feel for what happened in what order. I do not expect a second grader to remember everything I teach about Egypt, for instance. But when he studies the material again later, he will find himself in familiar territory. Thus he will have to memorize less because he will have some familiarity with the people and places involved.
    Textbooks, by themselves, teach you facts. They do not introduce you to real people. Teaching history to elementary school students should be like calling a child to storytime. You find a snug comfortable place, you curl up together, and you start with "Once upon a time . . ."

The Geography of Rome

1. Study a good relief map of Italy and Sicily.
    Locate any mountains, rivers, lakes, deserts.
    What are their names?

MOUNTAINS:	LAKES:
RIVERS:	**DESERTS:**
OCEANS/SEAS:	**OTHER:**

The Geography of Rome
(continued)

2. What major cities do you find?

_____

_____

_____

_____

3. Do the geographic features you listed divide the country into separated regions?

_____

_____

What features would provide natural defenses?

_____

_____

What areas of the country are more open to attack?

_____

_____

In what way?

_____

_____

The Geography of Rome
(continued)

4. Where would you expect food to be grown most easily?

    _____

    What other occupations would you expect to find in various regions of the country?

    _____

    _____

5. Take a piece of tracing paper and lay it over the relief map. Using a dark, soft lead pencil, trace the map of Italy. Be sure to include and label major mountains, rivers, lakes, deserts, and cities. Note significant features bordering the areas you are studying.

The Geography of Rome
(continued)

6. Make a salt map which shows the major features of Rome and Sicily.

    Step 1: On an unbendable piece of cardboard (about 15 x 15 inches), draw the outline of Rome and Sicily. Be sure and use a pencil.

    Step 2: Make the salt/flour dough
    1 part salt
    2 parts flour
    enough water to make a slightly sticky, but manageable dough
    (1 cup salt, 2 cups flour will make enough dough for two good sized maps.)
    If you would like to color the dough to show differences in elevation or vegetation, add a little food coloring or tempera paint to the dough when you add the water.
    Be sure to use a bowl that won't be stained by the dye.

    Step 3: Take the salt dough and press it into the outline you have drawn on the cardboard. Build up ridges for mountains, make depressions in the dough to show rivers, lakes or other low spots. You might want to use tempera paint to paint bordering oceans, nations, etc.

    Step 4: Lay map flat and let it dry overnight.

BACKGROUND STUDY

Suggested Reading: <u>The Aeneid for Boys and Girls</u> by Alfred Church
<u>City: A Story of Roman Planning and Construction</u> by David MacCaulay, and <u>The Romans</u> (Usborne Publishing).

<u>The Aeneid</u> is the story the Romans told about the ancestry of its founding Fathers. We read it in the children's version, <u>The Aeneid for Boys and Girls</u>, and I must confess, we found it to be a bit more difficult to read than the <u>Iliad</u> and the <u>Odyssey</u>. Actually my son balked. So I read the first few chapters aloud, stopping at the most suspenseful points I could find. Eventually, he got tired of waiting until the next day to find out what would happen, and I found him reading (and enjoying) it in bed one night. (I pretended to be surprised.) You may need to read it aloud to your students — breaking at points of suspense — and ease them into the story a bit. Younger students may need you to read all of it to them. Take your time and have fun with it.

Another book you may want to read is David Macaulay's <u>City</u>. How you assign this book will depend on the abilities and interests of your particular students. It can be used as background, or it can be read in conjunction with Chapter XIII on Appius Claudius Caecus, the great Roman builder.

Use the Reading Assignment sheet provided on the next page. Reproduce as many as you need and divide up the books into digestible chunks. Decide how much you will assign each day. It is possible to take spelling/vocabulary assignments from words found in the reading, as well.

Student _____ Date _____

READING ASSIGNMENT CHART

Topic _____

Book Titles:

(1) _____

(2) _____

(3) _____

Date	Book/Chapter	Pages

Copy as many of these as you need as you plan your study.

Chapter **I**

ROMULUS

Supplemental Texts:
The Romans, pages 4-5, "The Founding of Rome"

Vocabulary:

adjacent	descendants	stout
feeble	foundlings	prospered
resolved	erected	strode
patricians	plebeians	javelin
torrents		

People and Places:

Ae ne'as	Mediterranean Sea	Senate
Rom'u-lus	Re'mus	Ti'ber
Mars	Sa'bines	
Qui'ri-nus	Pal'en tine Hill	753 B.C.

For Discussion:

1. Note: The early history of a people is very often made up of mixtures of fact, myth and legend. Prepare students for this. Discuss the difference between the three. Factual things did happen. Legends are probably based on fact but have been exaggerated or mixed up with descriptions of things that are make-believe. There may have been a person named Romulus, but as more people told stories about him, the things that were true were exaggerated, and new adventures and abilities added, until it becomes difficult to separate truth from fiction. Myths did not actually happen but tell you something about what is important to the people who told them. This is a good time to discuss the uniqueness of the historical record of the Old Testament.

2. Tell the story of Romulus and Remus.

Chapter II

NUMA POMPILIUS

Vocabulary:

consult	augurs	manufacture
degraded	grove	grotto
induced	forge	quiver
prosperous	statuary	January

People and Places:

Nu'ma	E-ger'i-a	Ju'pi-ter
Ju'no	Nep'tune	Plu'to
Ha'des	Mars	Mer'cu-ry
Vul'can	A-pol'lo	Ja'nus
Phoe'bus	Di-an'a	Ve'nus
Flor'a	Min-er'va	

For Discussion:

1. How did Numa satisfy himself that he really should be ruling Rome? What does his desire to be <u>sure</u> that he was called to rule tell you about the type of person he was?

2. Before Numa, what had been the Romans' attitude toward work? How did Numa help to change that attitude?

3. Would you call Numa a religious man? Why or why not? In what did the Roman people generally believe?

4. Which god did the Romans chiefly honor? With this in mind, what would you expect the Roman nation to value?

5. Why was the door of the Temple of Janus open in wartime and closed in peace?

Chapter III

THE HORATII AND THE CURIATII

Vocabulary:

plunder	submit	petty
intense	anxious	pretence
throng	penance	

People and Places:

Ho-ra'ti-us	Ho-ra'ti-i	Cu-ri-a'ti-i
Al'bans		

For Discussion:

1. Why did the Romans declare war against each other?

2. Write a newspaper article that tells the story of the Horatii and the Curiatii. Write it up like the front page story of the <u>Roman Daily Times</u> (or whatever you wish to name your paper), or read it on tape as the lead story of a radio news broadcast.

Chapter IV

THE TARQUINS

Vocabulary:

engraved	ornamented	fasces
porticoes	sewer	census
pith	papyrus	cylindrical

People and Places:

O'sti-a	Lu-cu'mo	Tar'quin
For'um	Cir'cus Max'i-mus	Si'byl
Ser'vi-us Tul'li-us	Tar'quin the Proud	Ancus Marcius
Si'byl-line Books	Cap'i-to-line Hill	

For Discussion:

1. Ancus Marcius thought that it would help Rome to have a sea port. Why would access to a port be a help to Rome?

2. Discuss Lucumo's reaction to the "omen." What does his response show about his character? How is the Biblical principle, "He that is faithful over little shall be faithful over much" illustrated here?

3. Name several accomplishments of King Tarquin's reign.

4. Tell about King Tarquin's relationship with the augurs. What was their dispute over and how was it resolved?

5. How did Servius Tullius come to be king? Name three important things done by Servius Tullius during his reign. How did he die?

6. Tell about Tarquin the Proud and the Sibyl of Cumae. On what and on whom did the Roman rely for wisdom? Contrast this with the model of Solomon.

Chapter V

JUNIUS BRUTUS

Vocabulary:

simpleton	vow	avenge
eloquent	tyrant	banish
consul	melancholy	

People and Places:

Ju'ni-us Bru'tus	Sex'tus	Lu-cre'tia
Ti'tus and Ti-ber'i-us	E-tru'ri-a	E-trus'cans

For Discussion:

1. Pretend that you are a news reporter. Write a news story that might have appeared in the Roman Daily News about this time.

2. Describe Junius Brutus. What type of man would you say that he was?

3. What do you think about his response to his son's treason?

4. Tell how Junius Brutus died.

Chapter VI

HORATIUS

Vocabulary:
ward off

People and Places:
Ho-ra'tius   Ti'ber   Por-se'na
Sub'li-cian Bridge

For Discussion:

1. Tell the story of Horatius at the Sublician Bridge.

2. You might read Thomas Macaulay's (1800-1859) retelling of this story in the poem, "Horatius."

Chapter VII

MUCIUS THE LEFT-HANDED

Vocabulary:
concealed   mistook   fury
flinching

People and Places:
King Por-se'na   Ca'i-us Mu'cius

For Discussion:

Write a play dramatizing this story. You might want to record it on tape as a "radio drama," or perform it for friends or family.

(Our family had lots of fun with this one!)

Chapter VIII

CORIOLANUS

Vocabulary:

contempt   oppress   hardship
scarcity   proposed   veto
tribunes   cordially   hastened

People and Places:

Cai'us Mar'cius   Vol'scians
Cor'i-o-li   Cor'i-o-la'nus
Si'ci-ly

For Discussion:

1. Word Study: Show different words formed from "patri," meaning "father." PATRIcian, PATRIot, and PATRIotism are some examples.

2. How would you describe Coriolanus?

3. Describe the relationship between the patricians and the plebeians.

4. What did the plebeians do in an attempt to force the patricians to change?

5. Why did Coriolanus leave Rome?

6. When Coriolanus said, "You have saved Rome, but you have ruined your son" what did he mean? Why did he say it?

Chapter **IX**

THE FABII

Vocabulary:

spoils   earnest

People and Places:

Fa'bi-i   Quin'tus Fa'bi-us   River Cre-mer'a
Vei'i

For Discussion:

1. What were spoils? What did Quintus Fabius do with the spoils and what resulted from his actions?

2. Compare the actions of Quintus Fabius, Marcus Fabius and Caeso Fabius.

3. How did the Senate feel about the Fabii's concern for the plebeians? What did the Fabii decide to do and why?

4. Tell about the battle between the Fabii and the Veientians. Who won? Why do you think the Fabii offered to fight the Veientians?

5. How did the Veientians avenge themselves on the Fabii?

Chapter X

CINCINNATUS

Vocabulary:

dictator   pass under the yoke   hemmed in
taunted   jeered   subjugate
laurel wreath   laden

People and Places:

Lu'ci-us Quinc'ti-us   Cin-cin-na'tus
Al'ban Hills   Con'sul Mi-nu'cius

For Discussion:

1. How did this conflict between the Romans·and Aequians begin? How could the conflict have been avoided?

2. Describe the trick the Aequians played on the Romans. Was it successful?

3. When and why were dictators appointed? How do Roman dictators compare to Greek tyrants? (See "Pisistratus the Tyrant," Famous Men of Greece, page 68.)

4. What kind of person do you think Cincinnatus was? Why do you answer as you do?

5. Describe Cincinnatus' battle with the Aequians.

6. Draw a picture of the "yoke" conquered soldiers were required to walk under. How do you think they would feel as they passed under the yoke? What would make them feel that way? What do you think of the practice?

Chapter **XI**

CAMILLUS

Supplemental Texts:

The Romans, pages 50-51, "Education" (since the schoolmaster figures so prominently in one of this chapter's incidents)

Vocabulary:

carcass	besiege	scourge
ambassadors	compelled	clamber
aroused	woe	chasm

People and Places:

Mar'cus Fur'i-us	Ca-mil'lus
Fa-lis'ci-ans	Gauls
Bren'nus	Al'li-a
Mar'cus Man'li-us	Pon'tius Co-min'i-us
Quin'tus Sul-pi'tius	

For Discussion:

1. Tell how the Romans conquered the city of Veii.

2. How was an unworthy schoolmaster responsible for a peaceful end to the conflict between Falerii and Rome?

3. Why did Camillus leave Rome? What did he pray as he left? How were his prayers answered?

4. Where were the Gauls from? Describe them.
   What does their treatment of the old men in the Forum tell you about them?
   How did the geese save Rome?

5. Why was Camillus called the "Father of his Country?"
   Do you think he deserved the title? Why or why not?

Chapter XII

MANLIUS TORQUATUS

Supplemental Texts:

The Romans, pages 6-7, "The early Republic"

Vocabulary:

vessels	galleys	prows
rostrum	orators	

People and Places:

Man'li-i	Ti'tus Man'li-us
Mount Ve-su'vi-us	An'ti-um
Man'li-us Tor-qua'tus	

For Discussion:

1. How did Manlius Torquatus become a consul?

2. What was Manlius Torquatus' reputation? Do you think he deserved that reputation? Why or why not?

3. What does the word "rostrum" mean? Tell about the word's origin. How did it come to have its current meaning? Draw a picture of a Roman rostrum.

Chapter **XIII**

APPIUS CLAUDIUS CAECUS

Supplemental Texts:
City by David Macaulay
The Romans, page 18-19 & 70-73, "Roads," "Architecture," & "Building technology"

Vocabulary:
censor (Roman meaning)	public works	aqueduct
outrage	toga	savages
dignified	proposal	

People and Places:
Ap'pi-us Clau'di-us	Ap'pian Way
Ta-ren'tum	Post hu'mi-us
Pyr'rhus	

For Discussion:

1. What were Appius Claudius' greatest achievements?

2. How did the people of Tarentum feel about the Romans? How did they show their feelings? What was the result?

3. "The tongue of Cineas wins more cities than the sword of Pyrrhus." To what does this saying refer? What general applications does it have? Can you think of verses that express similar thoughts in <u>Proverbs</u>?

4. Tell about Appius' response to Cineas. What lessons can you learn from this story about Cineas?

Chapter XIV

REGULUS

Supplemental Texts:
The Romans, pages 8-9, "The expansion of Rome"

Vocabulary:
cultivated   boarding bridge   enraged
obliged

People and Places:
Pu'nic Wars   Car'thage   Pillars of Her-cu'les
Strait of Gi bral'tar   Phoe-ni'cian   Reg'u lus
First Punic War   241 B.C.   Xan-thip'pus

For Discussion:

1. What nations fought in the first Punic War? When was it fought? What does **Punic** mean?

2. Describe Carthage at the beginning of the first Punic War. Where was Carthage?

3. How did the war begin? Why did the Romans <u>say</u> they were fighting? Why do you think they said that?

4. How were the Romans at a disadvantage at the beginning of the war?

5. How did Regulus change the way the war was fought? Describe a boarding bridge. Explain how it worked.

6. How successful was Regulus' trip to Carthage?

7. Tell why his captors sent him back to Rome. What did he promise his captors before he left for Rome? Why did he leave the safety of Rome and return to Carthage?

8. Do you think Regulus was acting foolishly or honorably when he returned to Carthage?

Chapter XV

SCIPIO AFRICANUS

Vocabulary:

plebeians	aedile	magistrates
hastily	harass	throng
vanquished	compelled	

People and Places:

Pu'bli-us Cor-ne'lius	Scip'i-o A-fri-can'us	Spain
Han'nibal	Alps	Quint'tus Fa'bi-us
Fa'bi-an policy	Sy'phax	Has-dru'bal Gis'co
Sar-din'i-a	Si'ci-ly	202 B.C.

For Discussion:

1. When and how did the Second Punic War begin?

2. Describe Scipio Africanus. What kind of person do you think he was? Cite specific examples of his actions to support your answer.

3. Who was Hannibal? How did he feel about Rome? Why did he feel this way? Describe his campaign against Rome. Trace his route on a map.

4. What is a **Fabian policy**? How did this type of policy come to be called that?

5. Why did Scipio sail to Carthage?

6. Describe his battle with Numidia. Describe his battle with Hannibal.

7. How did Scipio and Hannibal feel about each other? What story is told about the two of them that illustrates this?

Chapter XVI

CATO THE CENSOR

Supplemental Texts:

The Romans, pages 10-11, "Rome's social and political structure"

Vocabulary:

stern   extravagance   degenerating
flourishing   arsenals   prosperous
envoys   armistice   embassy
scarce

People and Places:

Tus'cu-lum   Mar'cus Por'cius Ca'to
An-ti'o-chus   Pass of Ther-mop'y-lae
Paul'us Ae-mi'li-us   146 B.C.

For Discussion:

1. What kind of man was Cato the Censor?

2. What was a Roman censor? What does the word **censor** mean today? How might Cato's personality and policies have influenced the change in the word's meaning?

3. Why did Cato go to Carthage, and what did he find there? How did he feel about what he found? What did he do about it?

4. Why did Carthage go to war against Rome again? What was the outcome?

Chapter XVII

THE GRACCHI

Vocabulary:

tilled   resolved   spare

People and Places:

Grac'chi   Cor nel'i-a
Ti-ber'i-us Cai'us   Assembly of Tribes
At'ta-lus   Per'ga-mus
Ti'ber   121 B.C.

For Discussion:

1. How did Cornelia Gracchi feel about her two sons?

2. Why were the plebeians and the nobles in disagreement?
   Why is Tiberius Gracchi remembered as a champion of the poor?

3. Tell what happened to the two brothers.

Chapter XVIII

MARIUS

Supplemental Texts:
The Romans, pages 12-17, "The End of the Roman Republic," "The army," & "A soldier's life"

Vocabulary:

tribune	foul	barbarian
entrenched	abreast	gladiator
impudence	fertile	immense
reception	downcast	

People and Places:

Cai'us Mar'i-us	Ju-gur'tha	Teu'tons
Bal'tic Sea	Hel-ve'tia	Swit'zer-land
Arles	Rhone River	River Po
Sulla	Aix	Social War
Mith-ri-da'tes		

For Discussion:

1. From your reading, how would you describe Marius? What was his background? What offices did he hold? Why did the nobles not oppose him?

2. Against what peoples did Marius go to war?

3. Who were the barbarian people who invaded Rome? Where did they come from? What were they like?

4. What strategy did Marius use against them?

5. Describe Marius' battle against the Cimbri.

Chapter XVIII
MARIUS
(continued)

6. What was the **Social War**? What young noble rose to power through his participation in the Social War? How did Marius feel about him?

7. Describe the conflict between Sulla and Marius? What was the cause of it?

8. What circumstances led to Marius' return to Rome (during Sulla's war against Mithridates)? What did Marius do when he returned?

Chapter XIX

SULLA

Vocabulary:

ruddy	felix	fortified
proscription	anxiously	proscribed
massive	battering ram	

People and Places:

Ar-che-la'us	Cor-ne'li-i	Tri'umph
78 B.C.		

For Discussion:

1. Describe Sulla. Compare and contrast what you know about Sulla with what you know about Marius. What do the actions of the two men reveal about their characters?

2. Tell about Sulla's war with Mithridates. Where and why was it fought?

3. Tell how a battering ram worked. Draw a picture and demonstrate — or make a model and demonstrate. (However, we <u>strongly</u> suggest that the students do no structural damage, leaving all walls and doors intact.)

4. How did Sulla react to news of Marius' treatment of his friends and family in Rome?

5. Once Sulla was in control of Rome, what type of master did he prove to be?

Chapter **XX**

POMPEY THE GREAT

Supplemental Texts:

The Romans, pages 20-21, "Ships & shipping"

Vocabulary:

pirates   exhibitions
victor   ambitious

People and Places:

Pom'pey   Ju'li-us Cae'sar

For Discussion:

1. After Sulla's death, what new enemy to Rome arose?

2. How did Rome respond to this new enemy?

3. Describe Pompey. Why was he chosen to rid Roman territories of the pirates? How did he attempt to overcome them? How did this success lead to greater success?

4. In order to become master of Rome, Pompey set out to keep the people's favor. How did he do this? In what ways do you think leaders today follow in Pompey's footsteps?

5. Describe Pompey's Rome.

6. Who else wanted to be master of Rome? How did he and Pompey feel about each other?

Chapter **XXI**

JULIUS CAESAR

Supplemental Texts:

John Gunther, *Julius Caesar*, 1959, one of the Landmark Books

William Shakespeare, *Julius Caesar* (read it, listen to an audio tape, watch it on video, or see it performed live)!

The Romans, pages 28-29, "Sieges & fortifications"

Vocabulary:

legions	pilum	ballista
eagle bearer	disband	die (noun)
treacherously	dispatch	

People and Places:

Ju'li-us Cae'sar	Caesar's Commentaries
Ru'bi-con	Egypt
Phar-sa'li-a	Bru'tus
Mark An'to-ny	

For Discussion:

1. Tell about Julius Caesar's family. How did Caesar manage to survive Sulla's proscription lists?

2. Caesar was from a patrician family. How did the plebeians feel about him? Why did they feel the way they did?

3. What was Caesar's goal in life? Describe his progress toward the attainment of that goal. (Consider his life goals in an eternal perspective.)

4. Describe Caesar's time in Spain and Gaul. How did the time he spent there prepare him for later success?

Chapter XXI
JULIUS CAESAR
(continued)

5. Tell how the Roman army was organized. How did the soldier who served under Caesar feel about him? Why did they feel that way? What does that show about the type of man Caesar was? (You might ask your students to comment on whether this illustrates Caesar's virtue or his shrewdness)?

6. Remember that Pompey, in order to gain and retain power, set out to win the hearts of the Roman people. How did Caesar set out to win their hearts? What was Pompey's reaction to Caesar's actions?

7. What does the phrase "crossing the Rubicon" mean? How did it come to have that meaning?

8. Describe Caesar's entrance into Rome. Describe his conflict with Pompey.

9. "Veni, Vedi, Vice," is often quoted when Caesar's name is mentioned. What is the origin of the phrase?

10. Describe the Triumph held for Caesar upon his return to Rome. What change was made in his title — no longer merely ruler of the Republic, but... At what times had a man been given the title of dictator and for how long was it granted?

11. How did Caesar improve Rome?

12. How did the people of Rome generally feel about having kings rule them again? Relate this to the reading you did about the Tarquins. How did Caesar respond to those who dared to call him king? How did this dispute lead to Caesar's death?

13. Why did Caesar say "Et tu Brute?" as he was being attacked? What did he mean by it?

14. Why did Caesar's assassins tell the people they had to kill Caesar? What did the people think of their reasons? How did Mark Antony influence them?

15. If you have enough children studying this chapter, the murder scene from Shakespeare's <u>Julius Caesar</u> is a fun one to act out. Drape everyone in togas (Bible characters wear bathrobes and towels, Romans wear bed sheets)! Be sure and tell them to "Beware the Ides of March!" (That's March 15th, by the way).

Chapter **XXI**

CICERO

Supplemental Texts:

The Romans, pages 74-75, "The legal system"

Vocabulary:

prominent   oratory   intellectual
defied   conspirator

People and Places:

Mar'cus Tul'li-us Ci'ce-ro   Cat'i-line
Ful'vi-a   Ap'en-nines   Tri-um'vi-rate

For Discussion:

1. What is Cicero famous for? (Note: Cicero was a master of <u>Latin</u> style. Unfortunately his mastery is not so evident in English translations. If you read his speeches in English, you are likely to wonder what all the fuss is about.)

2. Tell the story of Cicero's conflict with Senator Catiline.

3. How did Antony feel about Cicero? How did Antony eventually act on those feelings?

Chapter **XXIII**

AUGUSTUS

Supplemental Texts:
The Romans, pages 22-23, "From republic to empire"

Vocabulary:

intimate	triumvirate	interfere
deserted	asp	imposing
distribute		

People and Places:

Oc-ta'vi-us	Mark An'to-ny	Le-pi'dus
Au-gus'tus	Sex'tus Pom'pey	Cle-o-pa'tra
Ac'ti-um	Prae-tor'i-an Guard	Hor'ace
Vir'gil	Liv'y	Ov'id
Pal'es-tine	Ju-de'a	

For Discussion:

1. What was the Triumvirate? How did it come into being?

2. If you were Octavius, Lepidus, or Antony, what would you hope to gain from participation in the Triumvirate? What would you need to beware of? Why?

3. Tell how the Triumvirate fell apart.

4. Describe Octavius. What kind of man was he? What do you think it would have been like to live under his rule?

5. In the Old Testament books of <u>Kings</u> and <u>Chronicles</u>, the kings of Israel and Judah are described and evaluated according to God's standard. How do you think Augustus would be described according to that standard?

Chapter XXIV

NERO

Suggested Reading:

Foxes' Book of Martyrs gives accounts of those who were martyred for their faith in Christ. The earliest stories included tell of those who were Martyred during Roman times. You will want to read this book first and decide how much, and in what way, you will pass the information on to your students. The descriptions of the things that happened to these believers are not pleasant reading and may be too intense/upsetting for younger students. However, it should be possible to tell the stories of some of these believers in a way that conveys the essentials of the story, including details appropriate for the individual students.

The Romans, pages 24-25, "The early Empire"

Vocabulary:

affectionate	warrant	deceived
caressed	troop	persecute

People and Places:

Ti-ber'i-us	A-grip-pi'na	Clau'di-us
Ca-lig'u-la	Bri-tann'i-cus	Lo-cus'ta
Lu'ci-an	Sen'e-ca	

For Discussion:

1. How would you describe Nero? Does he remind you of any of Israel's kings? Which?

2. Nero provides an excellent opportunity to discuss the reasons for including study of wicked men in study of History. What can we learn from studying Nero? What would be lost if we just skipped Nero and told only the stories of noble Romans?

Chapter **XXV**

TITUS

Vocabulary:

glutton amphitheater colossus
colossal sham

People and Places:

Gal'ba Vi-ttel'li-us Ves-pas'ian
Ti'tus Fla'vi-us Palestine` Jerusalem
Colosseum Pom'peii Mount Ve-su'vi-us

For Discussion:

1. Three things happened during this period that would make good topics for possible additional study:

   First, Mount Vesuvius erupted and destroyed the city of Pompeii. Your public library should have children's books on this topic. Videos may also be available. A parallel study of volcanoes might be conducted.

   Secondly, under Vespasian, Jerusalem was destroyed (70 A.D.), fulfilling Jesus' prophecy. You should refer your students to related biblical passages. (One of the arguments given to support an early completion of the New Testament is that not one book of the New Testament mentions the destruction of the Temple. This fact is strong evidence that all the books of the New Testament were written before 70 A.D.)

   Thirdly, following the destruction of Jerusalem, the Zealots took refuge in the fortress at Masada. Josephus, the Jewish historian (whose desire to please the Romans may have colored his perspective on things) tells this story. It is worth researching and including in your study.

Chapter XXV
TITUS
(continued)

2. Describe the Colosseum. Tell what it was used for.

3. Fill in the blanks below with the correct emperor.
   Titus   Vespasian   Vittellius

   a. Coliseum and baths finished under _____.

   b. Jerusalem destroyed under _____.

   c. _____ was a glutton.

   d. _____ was a former general who was sent to Rome by Nero
   to punish the Jews in Palestine.

   Answers: a. Titus   b. Vespasian   c. Vittelius   d. Titus

4. The things that entertain a people often tell much about their character and their
   values. What type of things entertained the Roman people? What conclusions can
   you draw about the nation's character and values? You might extend the
   discussion by asking the same questions about our own country.

Chapter **XXVI**

TRAJAN

Supplemental Texts:

The Romans, pages 52-55, "Jobs and occupations," & "Money and trade"

Vocabulary:

vassal

People and Places:

Do-mi'tian	Tra'jan	Rhine
Colonia	Cologne	Germany
Danube	Da'cia	De-ce'ba-lus
Ar-men'i-a	Trajan's Column	Me-so-po-ta'mi-a
Asia Minor	Ta'ci-tus	
Plu'tarch's Lives	Plu'tarch	

For Discussion:

1. What were Trajan's main accomplishments.

2. How did the Roman people feel about Trajan? From the reading you have done, what did the Romans seem to value in a leader.

3. The Romans often said that they wished for an emperor who would be as great as and as <u>GOOD</u> as . Do you agree with their assessment of Trajan?

Chapter XXVII

MARCUS AURELIUS

Supplemental Texts:

The Romans, pages 56-59, "Entertainments," & "Races and games"

Vocabulary:

engaged	stoics	doctrine
idle	courtiers	homage
accurate	hemmed in	industrious
dictate	statuary	

People and Places:

Ha'dri-an	Hadrian's Mole	Castle of St. Angelo
Ca'ta-combs	An-to'ni-us Pi'us	Mar'cus Au-re'li-us
Par'thi-a (modern day Iran)	Austria	Hungary
Qua di	Thundering Legion	Cas'sius

For Discussion:

1. How would you describe Hadrian? What was the purpose of Hadrian's Wall?

2. How were the Christians treated at this time? Where did they meet? How were they treated under Antonius Pius?

3. Who was Verus? What was his position? How did he get that position? Describe him. Compare him with Marcus Aurelius.

4. What kind of example did Marcus Aurelius set for the Roman people?

5. What were the Stoics? What did they teach?

6. What was the "Thundering Legion." How did it get its name? How did Marcus Aurelius feel about Christianity?

7. What did Cassius attempt to do? Describe what happened. What does Aurelius' treatment of Cassius tell about Aurelius?

Chapter **XXVIII**

DIOCLETIAN

Supplemental Texts:

The Romans, pages 26-27, 60-61, & 76-77, "The Administration of the empire," "The baths," & "The later empire"

Vocabulary:

bribes	corrupt	vice emperor
capable	endure	

People and Places:

Di-o-cle'tian	Max-im'i-an	Con'stan-tine
Edict of Prices		

For Discussion:

1. Casio Dio said "Our history and the affairs of the Romans descend from an age of gold to one of iron and rust." What did he mean and why did he say it? Do you agree with him?

2. What changes did Diocletian make in the Roman government? Why did he make them, and what were their effects? How well did they work?

3. How were Christian believers treated under Diocletian?

4. What was the "Edict of Prices?" How well did it work?

5. Diocletian felt that the Empire was too large to be ruled by one man. Do you think this was an accurate observation or an excuse for his failures? Defend your answer.

Chapter **XXIX**

CONSTANTINE THE GREAT

Supplemental Texts:
The Romans, pages 62-65, "Religious beliefs," & "Gods and goddesses"

Vocabulary:
expedient

People and Places:
Con'stan-tine	Tur'in	Eu-se'bi-us
La-bar'um	Thrace	Con'stan-ti-no-ple

For Discussion:

1. How did Constantine become emperor?

2. What story is told about Constantine's conversion?

3. In what way did Constantine's conversion bring relief to the Christians? What possible problems might come when it is suddenly popular (and politically expedient) to be a Christian?

4. Why did the people call Constantine "The Founder of Our Peace?"

5. Describe the relationship between Constantine and Licinius.

6. Why did Constantine move the capitol of the Empire? Find Constantinople (Now called Istanbul) on a map. See if you agree with his decision.

Chapter **XXX**

END OF THE WESTERN EMPIRE

Supplemental Texts:

The Romans, pages 78-80, "The Empire after Constantine," & "The Byzantine Empire"

Vocabulary:

reprimanded	barbarous	simpleton
exploits	subsequently	grandeur
sultan		

People and Places:

Julian	The-o-do'sius	Thes-sa-lo-ni'ca
Am'brose	Goths	Vandals
Britain	By'zan-tine Empire	O'do-a-cer
Ot'to-man Empire	Turkey	An'ka-ra

For Discussion:

1. What was Julian called? What was he primarily known for? Tell about his death. What might Julian have meant by his dying words?

2. How did Theodosius become Emperor of the East and West?

3. You receive an invitation from Theodosius to attend the circus at Thessalonica. Would you be wise to accept? Explain your answer.

4. Emperor Theodosius receives a message from Bishop Ambrose. What does it say? How does Theodosius respond?

5. Describe the shrinking of the Empire. Why and how did this happen?

6. What was the Byzantine Empire, and how did it get its name?

Summary Questions

1. Roman history can be divided into three general periods: Kingdom, Republic and Empire. Name one notable ruler from each period. Tell how they were significant.

2. What was your favorite story in Roman history?

3. Who do you think was Rome's best ruler? Her worst? Why do you pick these men?

CHRONOLOGICAL OVERVIEW
OF ROMAN HISTORY

B.C.

3000-1400	Minoan Culture dominates Greece 2700-2200:Old Kingdom in Egypt 2130-1800: Middle Kingdom in Egypt 1575-1100: New Kingdom in Egypt
1600-1150	Mycenaean Culture dominates Greece
1200	Fall of Troy
1200-900	Barbarian invasions in Greece Greek settlement of Aegean islands and west coast of Asia Minor Israelites first settle in Canaan 1000-960: King David 960-931: King Solomon
753	TRADITIONAL DATE FOR THE FOUNDING OF ROME
753-509	ROMAN KINGDOM (i.e. Rome ruled by kings)
715-672	NUMA POMPILIUS
593	(Solon's reforms in Athens)
534-509	TARQUINIUS SUPERBUS Roman Forum drained
519-439	CINCINNATUS
509	FOUNDATION OF THE REPUBLIC JUNIUS BRUTUS, consul First treaty with Carthage Horatius Mucius the Left-handed
508	(Clistenes rules Athens)
500	Coriolanus (500-450) The Fabii (500-450)
496	Latins defeated at battle of Lake Reguillus Treaty with Latins

CHRONOLOGICAL OVERVIEW OF ROMAN HISTORY
(continued)

461-430   (Pericles in power in Athens
        Sophocles
        Euripides
        The Sophists)

431-404   (Peloponnesian War)

405-396   SIEGE AND CAPTURE OF VEII

404-371   (Spartan preeminence in Greece)

399   (Execution of Socrates)

393   (Long Walls of Athens rebuilt)

390   SACK OF ROME BY THE GAULS

371-362   (Theban preeminence in Greece)

365   DEATH OF CAMILLUS

366   First plebeian consuls

340   Latin War

338   Campania incorporated into Roman state

359-336   (Philip of Macedonia in control of Greece)

336-323   (Alexander the Great)

323-276   (Wars for control of parts of Alexander's kingdom)
        (Alexander's kingdom divided between Seleucus, Antigonus, and Ptolemy I)

310   Rome begins to rule Etruria

280   APPIUS CLAUDIUS CAECUS dies
        Pyrrhus is defeated by Rome when he attempts to aid Greek cities in Sicily and Italy

270   Rome in control of all Greek cities in Italy

264   FIRST PUNIC WAR
        Rome acquires most of Sicily, also moves to control Corsica and Sardinia

CHRONOLOGICAL OVERVIEW OF ROMAN HISTORY
(continued)

263	Hiero of Syracuse allies self with Rome
256	Regulus sails to Africa
250	REGULUS dies
241	First Punic War ends
234-149	SCIPIO AFRICANUS
227	Sicily and Sardinia become Roman Provinces
221	HANNIBAL commands Carthaginian forces in Spain
219	Hannibal captures Saguntum (Roman ally) in Spain
218	SECOND PUNIC WAR BEGINS
217	Hannibal invades Italy
216	Hannibal defeats Romans at Cannae
215	Hannibal arrives in Southern Italy, Rome begins to gain ground in Spain, Carthage makes alliance with Syracuse
213	Rome besieges Syracuse (falls in 211)
211	Hannibal marches on Rome
211-206	SCIPIO AFRICANUS defeats Hasdrubal in Spain
204	SCIPIO invades Africa
203	Hannibal called back to Carthage
202	Scipio defeats Hannibal at Zama, Carthage becomes subject of Rome
197-133	Wars in Spain
184	Cato elected Censor
167	Direct taxation of Roman citizens abolished
155-86	MARIUS
149-146	Carthage destroyed by Rome, Africa becomes a Roman province Macedonia becomes Roman province

CHRONOLOGICAL OVERVIEW OF ROMAN HISTORY
(continued)

133	TIBERIUS GRACCHUS becomes Tribune
123-122	CAIUS GRACCHUS becomes Tribune
121	Massacre of Gracchan supporters authorized
112-106	Marius defeats Jugurtha of Mauretania
107-100	Marius elected consul six times, reforms army
106	CICERO born
102-101	Marius defeats Teutons and Cimbri
100	JULIUS CAESAR born
99	Lucretius born
91-88	SOCIAL WAR
88	SULLA marches on Rome
88-85	Mithridates VI attempts to free Greeks from Rome, slaughters Roman citizens in Asia
87	Marius seizes Rome
86	Marius dies SULLA captures Athens and Greece
83-82	Sulla returns to Italy, civil war follows Second war against Mithridates
82	Sulla appointed dictator of Rome
81	Cicero's earliest existing speech given
80	Sulla resigns
78	Sulla dies
73-71	SPARTACUS — Slave Revolt
74-63	Third war against Mithridates
70	Consulate of Crassus and POMPEY
66-63	Pompey defeats Mithridates Seleucid monarchy ends

CHRONOLOGICAL OVERVIEW OF ROMAN HISTORY
(continued)

63	Consulate of Cicero Catilinarian conspiracy
62	Pompey returns to Italy
60	FIRST TRIUMVIRATE FORMED
58-57	Period during which Cicero is exiled
58-49	Julius Caesar in Gaul
58-42	Julius Caesar writes <u>Gallic Wars</u>
55-54	Caesar's invasions of Britain
49	CAESAR CROSSES THE RUBICON, Civil War results
48	Caesar defeats Pompey at Pharsalus Pompey murdered in Egypt
47-44	Julius Caesar — Dictator of Rome
44	Caesar murdered on March 15th, (The Ides of March)
44	MARK ANTONY, consul, controls Rome Cicero attacks Antony in <u>Philippi</u>
43	OCTAVIAN (later Caesar Augustus) seizes the consulate Cicero murdered Ovid born SECOND TRIUMVIRATE: Antony, Lepidus, Octavian Opponents of Triumvirate murdered
42	Those who supported return to the Republic defeated at Philippi Cassius and Brutus commit suicide
37	Triumvirate renewed
31	Octavian defeats Antony at Actium
30	Antony and Cleopatra commit suicide Egypt becomes part of Rome
27	Octavian given title, "Augustus"
27-19	Agrippa conquers the rest of Spain

CHRONOLOGICAL OVERVIEW OF ROMAN HISTORY
(continued)

9	Rhine becomes a Roman frontier
@3-2	Birth of Jesus

A.D.

14-37	TIBERIUS
37-41	CALIGULA
41-54	CLAUDIUS
43	Aulus Pautius invades Britain
49	SENECA appointed to tutor Nero
54-68	NERO
59	Nero orders the murder of his mother, Agrippina
64	Rome burns for nine days, Christians persecuted
66-73	Jewish Revolt
67	Josephus, one of the leaders of the Jewish rebels, defects to Rome. Later writes a history of the period
69	FOUR EMPERORS: GALBA, OTHO, VITTELLIUS and VESPASIAN
69-79	VESPASIAN
70	TEMPLE AT JERUSALEM DESTROYED
73	Masada
79-81	TITUS
79	POMPEII and Herculaneum destroyed by eruption of MT VESUVIUS
81-96	DOMITIAN
98-117	TRAJAN
101-106	Trajan conquers Dacia (Romania) Mesopotamia and Armenia become part of the Empire

CHRONOLOGICAL OVERVIEW OF ROMAN HISTORY
(continued)

115-117	2nd Jewish Revolt
117-138	HADRIAN Hadrian's Wall built in Britain
138-161	ANTONINUS PIUS
161-180	MARCUS AURELIUS Plague spreads throughout Empire
165	Justinian martyred
229	Cassio Dio: "Our history and the affairs of the Romans descend from an age of gold to one of iron and rust"
249-51	Christians persecuted under Decius
284-306	DIOCLETIAN
303-305	GREAT PERSECUTION
306-337	CONSTANTINE Christianity declared to be the official religion of Rome
324	Constantinople founded
360-363	JULIAN THE APOSTATE
378-395	THEODOSIUS THE GREAT
410	ALARIC THE VISIGOTH sacks Rome
430	Augustine dies
439	Vandals conquer Carthage and Africa
476	End of the Western Roman Empire
527-565	JUSTINIAN, Emperor of the Eastern Empire, attempts to regain control of Italy and Africa
633-655	Arabs conquer Syria and Egypt
1453	Constantinople falls to the Turks End of the Eastern Roman Empire

A Few Words About Greenleaf Press

Greenleaf Press was founded by Rob & Cyndy Shearer in 1989. It was born of their frustration in searching for a history program for their children that was at the same time challenging, interesting, and historically accurate. What they were looking for was a curriculum that would begin at the beginning and present history in a logical, readable, chronological way. None of the available, in-print programs satisfied them. They discovered that the best history books for children they could find were, sadly, out of print. The best of the out-of-print classics were really terrific. They told interesting stories about real people. And the Shearer's discovered that their children loved history when it was presented in the form of an interesting story about a real person.

And so, they founded Greenleaf Press — to bring back to life some of the wonderful biographies which had been used to teach history so successfully in the past. The reprinting of Famous Men of Greece and Famous Men of Rome were Greenleaf's first publications. Those two books have now been joined by the reprint of Famous Men of the Middle Ages, Famous Men of the Renaissance and Reformation (written by Rob Shearer), The Greenleaf Guide to Old Testament History (written by Rob and Cyndy Shearer), and The Greenleaf Guide to Ancient Egypt (written by Cyndy Shearer).

Shortly after reprinting Famous Men of Rome, faced with questions from many people who liked the Famous Men books, but wanted help in HOW to use them, they decided to publish Study Guides showing how to integrate biographies, activities, and reference material. There are Greenleaf Guides available for Rome, Greece, and the Middle Ages, all written by Rob & Cyndy Shearer.

From that day to this, Greenleaf Press has remained committed to "twaddle-free", living books. We believe that history is both important and exciting and that our kids can share that excitement. We believe that if our children are to understand the roots of our modern-day, mixed-up world, they must study history. We're also thoroughly convinced that studying history with our children provides us with a wonderful opportunity to reflect with them on moral choices and Godly character.

Teaching History with Greenleaf Press Curriculum

Seven Year Plan

1st Year —	Old Testament (Historical Books: Genesis – Kings)
2nd Year —	Egypt (& Old Testament Review)
3rd Year —	Greece and Rome
4th Year —	The Middle Ages and The Renaissance
5th Year —	The Reformation and The Seventeenth Century (to 1715)
6th Year —	1715 to 1850
7th Year —	1850 to The Present

Six Year Plan

1st Year —	Old Testament and Egypt
2nd Year —	Greece and Rome
3rd Year —	The Middle Ages and The Renaissance
4th Year —	The Reformation to 1715
5th Year —	1715 to 1850
6th Year —	1850 to The Present

Five Year Plan

1st Year —	Old Testament, Egypt, Greece & Rome
2nd Year —	The Middle Ages and The Renaissance
3rd Year —	The Reformation and The Seventeenth Century (to 1715)
4th Year —	1715 to 1850
5th Year —	1850 to The Present

Four Year Plan

1st Year —	Old Testament, Egypt, Greece & Rome
2nd Year —	The Middle Ages, The Renaissance, and The Reformation
3rd Year —	1600 to 1850
4th Year —	1850 to The Present

Internet: www.greenleafpress.com
3761 Highway 109 N., Unit D
Lebanon, TN 37087
615-449-1617

Teaching History with Living Books
An overview of
GREENLEAF PRESS
Study Guides and History Packages

The Greenleaf Guide to Old Testament History

We are strongly persuaded that the history of Israel ought to be the first history studied by every child. This Guide outlines a daily reading program that works through all of the historical books of the Old Testament. The focus is on history — not theology. What is remarkable is that the historical books of the Bible always focus on a central character. The pattern of history in the Old Testament is built around a series of biographies and character studies. The Old Testament really could be subtitled "Famous Men of Israel." Thus, the Study Guide discussion questions focus on "What actions of this person are worthy of imitation?" "What actions should we avoid?" "What is God's judgment on this life?"

The 196 readings are intended to be used, one each day throughout the school year. Yes, we know that's a few more readings than most people have school days. Be creative. You could do more than one reading on some days, or you could continue the study into the summer or the next school year. The readings are designed to give the student (and parent/teacher) an overview of the history of Israel and an introduction to the key figures whose lives God uses to teach us about Himself and His character. These stories are intended for children in the elementary grades, and should be accessible, even to children in kindergarten or first grade (though they make a rich study for older children, even teens and adults)! If this seems surprising, the reader is reminded that God's plan for families is for fathers to teach these stories to their children. When God decrees in Deuteronomy 6:6-7 that "you shall teach them diligently to your sons and shall talk of them when you sit in your house and when you walk by the way and when you lie down and when you rise up," He is not referring to math facts and grammar rules. God's textbook for children are the stories from the Old Testament. He is specifically referring to the story of the Exodus from Egypt, but by implication He means the entire Old Testament. The Old Testament is God's textbook for children. This is the only textbook, quite probably, Jesus used during his education in the house of his parents. *Duration: One full academic year*

The Greenleaf Guide to Ancient Egypt

Ever wonder how Biblical history and Ancient Egypt fit together? Why was God so angry with Pharaoh anyway? This makes a perfect second history unit for students. Or, as an alternative, you could pause in your study of Old Testament history and study Egypt after you have finished the story of Joseph at the end of the book of Genesis. This unit has ten lessons, including one devoted to the rediscovery of Egypt and the development of the science of archaeology in the 19th century. There is also a lesson on the Exodus in the context of Egyptian culture. The main text for the study is the Landmark book, <u>The Pharaohs of Ancient Egypt</u>, which includes biographies of the following Pharaohs:

Cheops (builder of the Great Pyramid)
Hatshepsut (His Majesty, Herself!)
Thutmose III (the Napoleon of the
  Ancient World)

Aknaton (the monotheistic Pharaoh)
Tutankamon (the boy-Pharaoh)
Rameses II (Smiter of the Asiatics)
Duration: approximately 15 weeks

Famous Men of Greece

If you were to have asked a citizen of ancient Greece to tell you something about the history of his nation, he would have wanted to begin at what he would have considered to be the beginning. He would have begun by telling you about his gods and the myths and legends told about them. Even though the events described in the myths did not actually happen in the way the story says, the Greek myths will tell you much about what was important to the people who told them.

Greek culture forms the backdrop to all the events of the New Testament. Paul was educated not just in the teachings of the Rabbis, but also in the writings of the Greeks. He was able to quote from literature in his speech to the men of Athens. Many of the details in his letters become richer and more significant when understood in the context of Greek culture.

Famous Men of Greece covers the following chapters:

Introduction: the Gods of Greece	Lycurgus	Socrates
Deucalion and the Flood	Draco and Solon	Xenophon
Cadmus and the Dragon's Teeth	Pisistratus the Tyrant	Epaminondas and Pelopidas
Perseus	Miltiades the Hero of Marathon	Philip of Macedonia
Hercules and His Labors	Leonidas at Thermopylae	Alexander the Great
Jason and the Golden Fleece	Themistocles	Demosthenes
Theseus	Aristides the Just	Aristotle, Zeno, Diogenes, Apelles
Agamemnon, King of Men	Cimon	Ptolemy
Achilles, Bravest of Greeks	Pericles	Pyrrhus
The Adventures of Odysseus	Alcibiades	Cleomenes III
	Lysander	*Duration: approximately 15 weeks*

Famous Men of Rome

Rome was the political super-power of the ancient world. Rome history spans 500 years as a kingdom, 500 years as a Republic, and 500 years as an Empire (when Rome was ruled by military dictators who called themselves "Caesar"). It was the Pax Romana of the Empire that allowed the Gospel to spread rapidly to every corner of the earth. And it was the example of the Roman Republic which inspired the United States' Founding Fathers.

Famous Men of Rome covers the following individuals:

Romulus	Cincinnatus	Julius Caesar
Numa Pompilius	Camillus	Cicero
The Horatii and the Curiatii	Manlius	Augustus
The Tarquins	Manlius Torquatus	Nero
Junius Brutus	Appius Claudius Caecus	Titus
Horatius	Regulus	Trajan
Mucius the Left-Handed	Scipio Africanus	Marcus Aurelius
Coriolanus	Cato the Censor	Diocletian
The Fabii	The Gracchi	Constantine the Great
	Marius	End of the Western Empire
	Sulla	
	Pompey the Great	*Duration: approximately 15 weeks*

Famous Men of the Middle Ages

We come to a time when the power of Rome was broken and tribes of barbarians who lived north of the Danube and the Rhine took possession of the lands that had been part of the Roman Empire. These tribes were the Goths, Vandals, Huns, Franks and Anglo-Saxons. From the mixture of Roman provinces, Germanic tribes, and Christian bishops came the time known as The Middle Ages and the founding of the European nation-states.

Famous Men of the Middle Ages covers the following individuals:

The Gods of the Teutons
The Niebelungs
Alaric the Visigoth
Attila the Hun
Genseric the Vandal
Theodoric the Ostrogoth
Clovis
Justinian the Great
Two Monks: Benedict
    and Gregory
Mohammed
Charles Martel
Charlemagne
Harun-al-Rashid
Egbert the Saxon

Rollo the Viking
Alfred the Great
Henry the Fowler
Canute the Great
El Cid
Edward the Confessor
William the Conqueror
Gregory VII & Henry IV
Peter the Hermit
Frederick Barbarossa
Henry the Second and
    His Sons
Louis the Ninth
St. Francis and St. Dominic
Robert Bruce

Marco Polo
Edward the Black Prince
William Tell
Arnold Von Winkelried
Tamerlane
Henry V
Joan of Arc
Gutenberg
Warwick the Kingmaker

Duration: approximately 15 weeks (though many families supplement this study with literature readings and extend it to a full year).

Famous Men of the Renaissance and Reformation

The Middle Ages were not the "Dark Ages." Yet there had been substantial changes in Europe from 500 to 1300 AD. Rome and her Empire fell. The Germanic tribes moved into the old Roman provinces and established feudal kingdoms. Many of the Roman cities declined in population or were abandoned. Gradually, much of the literature and learning of the classical world was lost and forgotten. Around 1300, in the towns of northern Italy especially, a group of men began to devote themselves to the recovery and revival of the classical world.

As the men of the Renaissance completed their work of recovery, another group of men arose, devoted to reform of the abuses within the church and relying upon the texts and tools of scholarship developed by the Renaissance humanists. The Protestant Reformation marks the beginning of "modern" European history. During that time we see men and women of remarkable courage and ability devoted to restoring the church to Biblical patterns. There are triumphs and virtues to be imitated, and tragedies and vices to be avoided.

Famous Men of the Renaissance and Reformation covers the following individuals:

Renaissance
Petrarch
Giotto
Filippo Brunelleschi and
    Donatello
Lorenzo Valla
Cosimo D' Medici
Lorenzo D' Medici
Girolamo Savonarola
Sandro Botticelli
Leonardo Da Vinci
Cesare Borgia

Niccolo Machiavelli
Leo X (Giovanni De Medici)
Albrecht Durer
Michelangelo Buonarroti
Erasmus
Reformation
John Wyclif
Jan Hus
Martin Luther
Charles V
Ulrich Zwingli
Thomas Muntzer

Conrad Grebel & Michael
    Sattler
Melchior Hoffman, Jan
    Matthys & Menno Simons
Henry VIII
Thomas More
William Tyndale
Thomas Cromwell & Thomas
    Cranmer
John Calvin
John Knox
Duration: Approximately 15 weeks

Graphical Timeline of Ancient History

by Robert G. Shearer
© 1996 Greenleaf Press

Key Dates
Israel

c.1900 B.C. –	Joseph sold into slavery
c.1445 B.C. –	The Exodus
c.1000 B.C. –	Death of Saul, David becomes King
605-536 B.C. –	The Exile

Egypt

2500 B.C. –	Khufu (Cheops) The Great Pyramid
1505-1484 B.C. –	Queen Hatshepsut
1361-1344 B.C. –	Amenhotep IV also known as Akhenaton
51-31 B.C. –	Cleopatra

Greece

c.1200 B.C. –	Siege of Troy
478-404 B.C. –	Civil War between Athens & Sparta
356-323 B.C. –	Alexander

Rome

753 B.C. –	Founding of Rome
509 B.C. –	Founding of the Roman Republic
100-44 B.C. –	Julius Caesar
312-327 A.D. –	Constantine
410 A.D. –	Sack of Rome by the Visigoths
476 A.D. –	Death of the last Roman Emperor

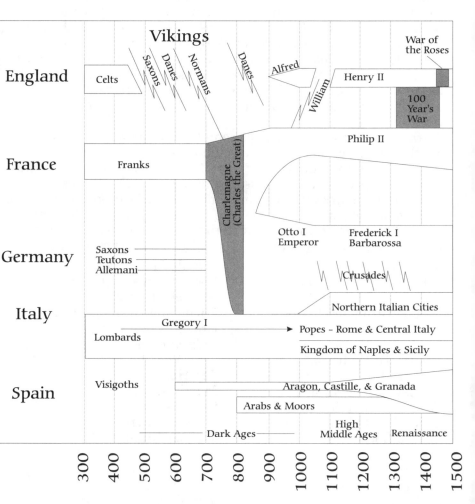

Graphical Timeline of Medieval History

Key Dates
England:

c.400 –	Romans withdraw
793 –	Sack of Lindisfarne by Vikings
871-899 –	Alfred the Great
1066 –	Norman Conquest
1339-1453 –	Hundred Years War
1455-1485 –	War of the Roses

France:

482-511 –	Clovis
714-41 –	Charles Martel
768-814 –	Charlemagne
1180-1223 –	Philip II Augustus
1412-1431 –	Joan of Arc

Germany:

936-937 –	Otto I, the Great
1152-90 –	Frederick I Barbarossa
1210-50 –	Frederick II, Stupor Mundi
1493-1519 –	Maximilian
1516-1556 –	Charles V

Italy:

440-461 –	Pope Leo I
480-543 –	St. Benedict
590-640 –	Pope Gregory
1073-85 –	Pope Gregory
1200-1240 –	St. Francis
1309-1378 –	Babylonian Captivity (of the Papacy)
1378-1417 –	The Great Schism
1096 –	1st Crusade
1147 –	2nd Crusade
1189 –	3rd Crusade